BABY JUDAH LEARNS TO INVEST
Children's Financial Literacy Series

Black Lion Incorporated
www.blacklionfoundation.com

Written by: James Holmes, Jr.
Illustrated by: King Larmie

Black Lion Owners, Kimberly & James Holmes

Black Lion Inc. is jointly owned by Kimberly Holmes and James Holmes, Jr. Kimberly has over 33 years experience as a licensed Attorney and James has over 35 years as a Finance, Investment and Credit Professional. Both are at the pinnacle of their chosen professions. Together they completely own and operate five different S-Corporations. All four of their millennial aged children are college graduates. To whom much is given, much is required.

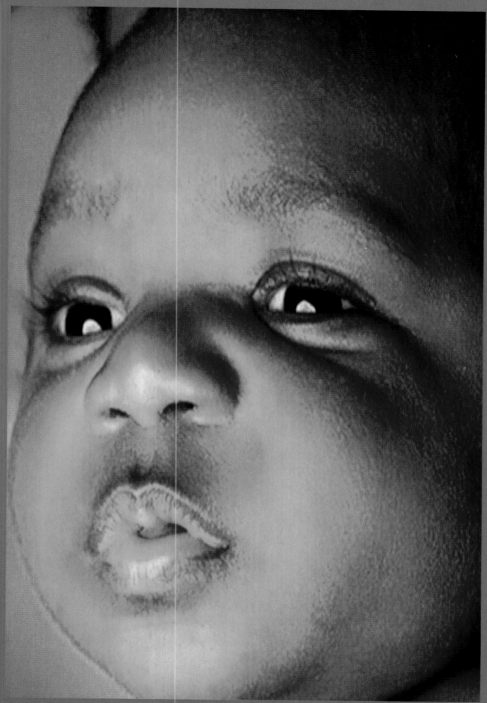

This book is inspired by and dedicated to our first born Grandchild. "Baby King Judah"!

"The wealthy teach their children how to acquire, the rich teach their children how to sell, and the poor teach their children how to buy."
-Eugene Mitchell

The contents of this book include various forms of graphics. The hand illustrations were created by King Larmie. At the time of this publication, he is a student at The FAIR School of Arts in Minneapolis.

A young smiling boy from Little Rock named Judah, lovingly referred to as "Baby King Judah" by Grand Daddy James. "Baby King Judah" was a happy and friendly young lad.

Grand Daddy James says it's because he prayed before Judah was born, that he would be healthy and happy.

Grand Daddy said God was particulalry generous when he made "Baby King Judah"!

Every time Grand Daddy James saw Judah, he would say encouraging words like, the world is yours, you can be whatever you want "Baby King"!

I can be anything Grand Daddy? Yes, "Baby King" you sure can!

What if I want to be a Doctor? It's yours, Grand Daddy James enthusiastically replied.

Judah asked, what if I want to be an engineer? Without hesitation, Grand Daddy responded, it's yours for the taking. Then the curious lad countered, what do engineers do?

After gathering and organizing his thoughts, Grand Daddy James advised, there are several different types of engineers: Mechanical Engineers help designed and build things, Chemical Engineers usually work with science and so forth. Then there are Software Engineers who usually work in technology related areas.

Do you mean companies like Amazon, Apple and Google?
Yes "Baby King", you are a quick learner! I have been using
advanced words and phases by design to stretch your
intellectual muscles since you were in the cradle. As of now, you
are even surpassing my lofty expectations!

Is that why you tell me I can be anything I want? Correct, Grand Daddy gleefully exclaimed. After they both laughed and hugged, Judah regrouped with another question. What if I want to be a Lawyer like Grand Mommy Kim?

Yes, you absolutely could be an Attorney like your Grand Mommy Kim! I know she would like that, said Grand Dadddy.

I have a tricky one for you now Grand Daddy. Could I own several businesses like you do? Grand Daddy James smugly said you already do "Baby King".

I don't understand , what do you mean, I already own companies?

Grand Daddy James explained, well "Baby Judah" the week you were born, I bought some stock for you. By owning stock in a company it means you actually own a small percentage of that company.

See here, as he pulled out the investment statement, you already own stock in several companies and they are growing, so your account will get bigger and bigger!

You are going to have a lot of nice financial options as you age and mature.

Thank you Grand Daddy, as "Baby King Judah" happily hugged his Grandfather!

Can we play the Investment game, Grand Daddy?
Ha...ha...ha...Grand Daddy gave a big laugh. I know why
you want to play the Investment Game. Because you
have been practicing so you can earn some dollars. Yes
Sir, said the eager lad, I have been practicing and
Momma and Dad have been helping me.

Okay "Baby King", here are the flash cards. Grand Daddy instructed, tell about "DIVERSIFICATION"?

"Baby King Judah" yelled out, not putting all my eggs in the same basket, as he did his special happy dance!

That's right "Baby King", here are $5 dollars.

Then Grand Daddy pursed his lips and popped off "DOLLAR COST AVERAGING"? After a brief pause...Judah replied, investing the same dollar amount every week or month, for example $25 dollars every week or $100 dollars every month. So, when the market is up you buy less shares and when it is down, you buy more shares

Then the little fella got really fancy when he chirped, that mitigates your risk, and commenced with another happy Judah dance. Wow! Grand Daddy stated, mitigating risk, such a fancy phase for a little tike! Judah piped, yes Momma taught me that one just to impress you. Grand Daddy responded sheepishly, I am impressed...not...overwhelmed...ha...ha...ha...but impressed...ha...ha...ha. They both laughed and hugged each other, amused at Grand Daddy's corny humor.

They laughed and had their own little party! They were buddies having fun learning cool stuff!

The time "Baby king Judah" spent practicing "THE INVESTMENT GAME" was paying off in dollars, just like life.

"Baby King" that was so impressive, let's double, you get $10 dollars for that one, then Grand Daddy quickly snuck in "COMPOUNDING INTEREST'? My interest on my interest adding up more and more the longer I keep it invested, gleefully stated the little dancer.

That's five more dollars "Baby King".

This is today's last flash card. What is "OPPORTUNITY COST"? This time Judah confidently started his happy dance before answering the question, he excitedly shouted, if I choose to buy Nike shoes with the money that I earn today, then I lose the opportunity to buy more toys.

Correct, said Grand Daddy, that's five more dollars.
What's your total for the day "Baby King"?

Judah counted the five dollar bills out loud, one...two...three...that's five, for a total of $25 dollars. Grand Daddy add, yes and a five dollar bonus for solving the math equation. The total now is $30 dollars.

Predictably, it was time for another Judah happy dance!

Judah expressed his gratitude by thanking his Grandfather, then energetically roared, I like "THE INVESTMENT GAME"! This is fun!

You get to spend it on anything you want, Grand Daddy James explained. Judah replied, I already have a lot of toys.

How many toys can a kid play with? Mused the young lad. I want to expand my thinking. I have to put on my big boy thinking hat.

Grand Daddy was humored and impressed by the young chap's oral reasoning.

"Baby King" continued to think out loud. Since I have an abundance of toys...Then Grand Daddy interrupted, there you go with those big words, little man...ha...ha...ha.

Then Judah piped out, I want to buy some more businesses, some more stocks!

Judah asked, can I do that with $30 dollars? Grand Daddy responded, not only can you, I am going to reward your wisdom by doubling it to $60 dollars. Let's buy them with my phone now.

Thank you Grand Daddy! As Judah jumped in his arms and gave him a big warm hug!

I guess I am off to a pretty good investment start for a young guy, right?

Grand Daddy ended by saying, that's right "Baby King", you are off to a wonderful start!

THE END

Special Acknowledgements to Baby King Judah's parents Zedric and Desirae. Thanks for sharing God's amazing gift!

Black Lion

Financial voice of the under served

Visit Black Lion's other companies:
WWW.BLACKLIONFOUNDATION.COM
WWW.SYNERGYDIVERSITY.COM
WWW.BLACKLIONINVESTS.COM
WWW.BLACKLIONAUTO.COM

Primary Author James Holmes, Jr. President of Black Lion Inc. has over 35 years of experience as a Finance, Investment and Credit specialist. After retiring from the Corporate Industry in 2019 ,James has made it his mission to mentor and train as many young minds as possible. Black Lion Inc. is dedicated to preparing them for a challenging world.

Made in the USA
Columbia, SC
18 May 2021